THE ANCIENT
SOUTH
ASIAN
= WORLD =

STUDENT STUDY GUIDE

OXFORD
UNIVERSITY PRESS

Oxford University Press, Inc., publishes works that
further Oxford University's objective of excellence
in research, scholarship, and education.

Oxford   New York
Auckland   Cape Town   Dar es Salaam   Hong Kong   Karachi
Kuala Lumpur   Madrid   Melbourne   Mexico City   Nairobi
New Delhi   Shanghai   Taipei   Toronto

With offices in
Argentina   Austria   Brazil   Chile   Czech Republic   France   Greece
Guatemala   Hungary   Italy   Japan   Poland   Portugal   Singapore
South Korea   Switzerland   Thailand   Turkey   Ukraine   Vietnam

Published by Oxford University Press, Inc.
198 Madison Avenue, New York, NY 10016
www.oup.com

ISBN-13: 978-0-19-522290-6 (California edition)   ISBN-13: 978-0-19-522166-4
ISBN-10: 0-19-522290-3   (California edition)   ISBN-10: 0-19-522166-4

Writer: Kimberley Houston
Editor: Monique Peterson
Project Editor: Lelia Mander
Project Director: Jacqueline A. Ball
Education Consultant: Diane L. Brooks, Ed.D.
Design: designlabnyc

Casper Grathwohl, Publisher

9 8 7 6 5 4 3 2 1
Printed in the United States of America
on acid-free paper

Dear Parents, Guardians, and Students:

This study guide has been created to increase student enjoyment and understanding of *The Ancient South Asian World*. It has been developed to help students access the text. As they do so, they can learn history and the social sciences and improve reading, language arts, and study skills.

The study guide offers a wide variety of interactive exercises to support every chapter. Parents or other family members can participate in activities marked "With a Parent or Partner." Adults can help in other ways, too. One important way is to encourage students to create and use a history journal as they work through the exercises in the guide. The journal can simply be an off-the-shelf notebook or three-ring binder used only for this purpose. Some students might like to customize their journals with markers, colored paper, drawings, or computer graphics. No matter what it looks like, a journal is a student's very own place to organize thoughts, practice writing, and make notes on important information. It will serve as a personal report of ongoing progress that your child's teacher can evaluate regularly. When completed, it will be a source of satisfaction and accomplishment for your child.

Sincerely,

Casper Grathwohl
Publisher

This book belongs to:

_____

CONTENTS

HOW TO USE THE
STUDENT STUDY GUIDES TO
THE WORLD IN ANCIENT TIMES

The World in Ancient Times will introduce you to some of the greatest civilizations in history, such as ancient Rome, China, and Egypt. You will read about rulers, generals, and politicians. You will learn about scientists, writers, and artists. The daily lives of these people were far different from your life today.

The study guides to The World in Ancient Times *will help you as you read the books. They will help you learn and enjoy history while building thinking and writing skills. They will also help you pass important tests and just enjoy learning. The sample pages below show the books' special features. Take a look!*

Before you read

- Have a notebook or extra paper and a pen handy to make a history journal. A dictionary and thesaurus will help you too.

- Read the two-part chapter title and predict what you will learn from the chapter.

- Quotation marks in the margin show the sources of ancient writings. The main primary sources are listed next to the chapter title.

- Study all maps and photos. Read the captions closely. (This caption tells that the statue itself is a primary source. Artifacts are records of history, just like writings.)

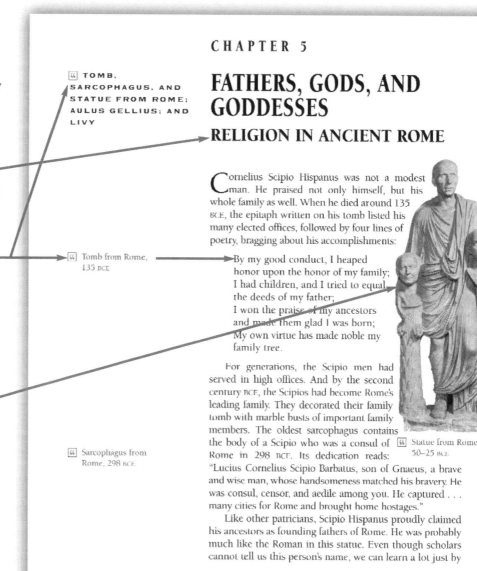

`❝` TOMB, SARCOPHAGUS, AND STATUE FROM ROME; AULUS GELLIUS; AND LIVY

`❝` Tomb from Rome, 135 BCE

`❝` Sarcophagus from Rome, 298 BCE.

CHAPTER 5
FATHERS, GODS, AND GODDESSES
RELIGION IN ANCIENT ROME

Cornelius Scipio Hispanus was not a modest man. He praised not only himself, but his whole family as well. When he died around 135 BCE, the epitaph written on his tomb listed his many elected offices, followed by four lines of poetry, bragging about his accomplishments:

By my good conduct, I heaped honor upon the honor of my family;
I had children, and I tried to equal the deeds of my father;
I won the praise of my ancestors and made them glad I was born;
My own virtue has made noble my family tree.

For generations, the Scipio men had served in high offices. And by the second century BCE, the Scipios had become Rome's leading family. They decorated their family tomb with marble busts of important family members. The oldest sarcophagus contains the body of a Scipio who was a consul of Rome in 298 BCE. Its dedication reads: "Lucius Cornelius Scipio Barbatus, son of Gnaeus, a brave and wise man, whose handsomeness matched his bravery. He was consul, censor, and aedile among you. He captured . . . many cities for Rome and brought home hostages."

Like other patricians, Scipio Hispanus proudly claimed his ancestors as founding fathers of Rome. He was probably much like the Roman in this statue. Even though scholars cannot tell us this person's name, we can learn a lot just by

`❝` Statue from Rome, 50–25 BCE.

As you read

- Keep a list of questions.

- Note **boldfaced** words in text. They are defined in the margins.
  Their *root words* are given in *italics*.

- Look up other unfamiliar words in a dictionary.

- Find important places on the map on pp. 12–13.

- Look up names in Cast of Characters on pp. 9–11 to learn pronunciation.

- Read the sidebars. They contain information to build your understanding.

After you read

- Compare what you have learned with what you thought you would learn before you began the chapter.

looking at him. First: he's a Roman. We know because he's wearing a toga, the garment that was a sign of manhood. The Romans called it the *toga virilis*, and a boy wasn't allowed to wear it until he became a man, usually at 16. Second, because this unknown Roman is carrying masks of his ancestors, we know that his father or grandfather had served as one of Rome's top officials.

These masks, made of wax or clay, usually hung in the hallways of the ancestral home. Romans took them down and carried them in parades and funeral processions.

Roman families were organized like miniature states, with their own religions and governments. The oldest man in the family was called the **paterfamilias**, the patriarch. He was the boss, and his words were law. Scipio Hispanus was the paterfamilias in his family. This meant that he held lifelong power, even over life and death. He could sell or kill a disobedient slave. He had the right to abandon an unwanted baby, leaving him or her outside to die. Usually this would be a sick child or a baby girl to whom the family couldn't afford to give a dowry when she grew up. Romans wanted healthy sons to carry on the family name, yet a father could imprison, whip, disown, or even execute a son who committed a crime. In 63 BCE, a senator named Aulus Fulvius did exactly that after his son took part in a plot to overthrow the government. But this didn't happen very often. Roman fathers were expected to rule their families with justice and mercy, the same way that political leaders were expected to rule the state.

For both the family and the state, religion played a major role in life. Every Roman home had a shrine to the household gods, the Lares. The father served as the family's priest. Scipio Hispanus would have led his family's prayers and made sacrifices to honor their ancestors and please the gods that protected the entire family—living and dead. When a baby was born, Scipio Hispanus would have hit the threshold of his home with an axe and a broom to frighten away any wild spirits that might try to sneak in. When a household member died, family members carried the body out feet first to make sure that its ghost didn't run back inside. (That's why people still sometimes describe death as "going out feet first.")

vir = "man"
Roman boys donned the *toga virilis* when they became men. *Virilis* is a form of *vir*; "virile" means "manly."

pater + familias = "father" + "family"
The paterfamilias was the oldest male member of a Roman family.

TOMBS OF THE SCIPIOS

The Romans believed that the dead should neither be buried nor cremated inside the city walls. They were afraid that Rome's sacred places would become polluted by the presence of death. So they lined the roads leading away from Rome with monuments built to house and honor the dead. Visitors can still see the tombs of the Scipios buried along the Appian Way, about two miles from the Forum. (The Appian Way is a military road that was built in the fourth century BCE.)

The next two pages have models of graphic organizers. You will need these to do the activities for each chapter on the pages after that.

Go back to the book as often as you need to.

GRAPHIC ORGANIZERS

As you read and study history, geography, and the social sciences, you'll start to collect a lot of information. Using a graphic organizer is one way to make information clearer and easier to understand. You can choose from different types of organizers, depending on the information.

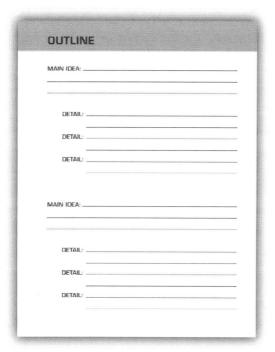

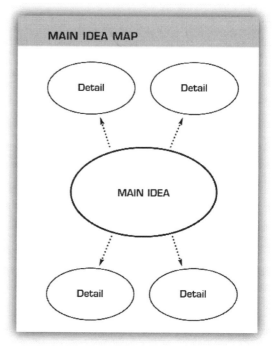

Outline

To build an outline, first identify your main idea. Write this at the top. Then, in the lines below, list the details that support the main idea. Keep adding main ideas and details as you need to.

Main Idea Map

Write down your main idea in the central circle. Write details in the connecting circles.

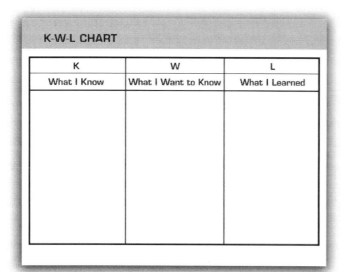

K-W-L Chart

Before you read a chapter, write down what you already know about a subject in the left column. Then write what you want to know in the center column. Then write what you learned in the last column. You can make a two-column version of this. Write what you know in the left and what you learned after reading the chapter.

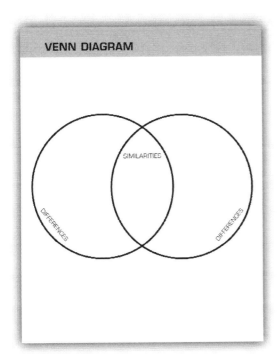

Venn Diagram

These overlapping circles show differences and similarities among topics. Each topic is shown as a circle. Any details the topics have in common go in the areas where those circles overlap. List the differences where the circles do not overlap.

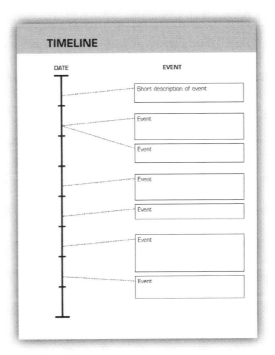

Timeline

A timeline divides a time period into equal chunks of time. Then it shows when events happened during that time. Decide how to divide up the timeline. Then write events in the boxes to the right when they happened. Connect them to the date line.

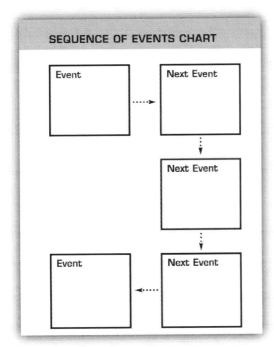

Sequence of Events Chart

Historical events bring about changes. These result in other events and changes. A sequence of events chart uses linked boxes to show how one event leads to another, and then another.

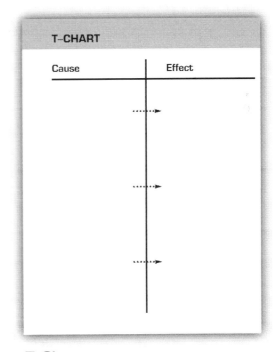

T–Chart

Use this chart to separate information into two columns. To separate causes and effects, list events, or causes, in one column. In the other column, list the change, or effect, each event brought about.

IMPORTANT VOCABULARY WORDS

The Word Bank section of each lesson will give you practice with important vocabulary words from the book. The words below are also important. They're listed in the order in which they appear in each chapter. Use a dictionary to look up any you don't know.

Chapter 1
mine
chalcedony
symbolize
mass
cultivate
earthquake
concrete
peninsula
tectonic plate
molten
landmass
barter
tropical
plateau

Chapter 2
glacial deposit
climate
fertile
memorize
equivalent
unfortunately
emerge
atomic analysis
invincible

Chapter 3
bitumen
harvest
sickle
bullock
nomad
experiment
kernel
channel
irrigation
intruder
bandit
humankind
agriculture

Chapter 4
vessel
silty
knead
socket
artisan
bonfire
kiln
figurine
deposit
deforest
terracotta

Chapter 5
abandoned
littered
evidence
failure
legacy
ordinary
mortar
maintain
impressions
dissolve
cinders
furnaces
afford
tributaries

Chapter 6
hesitate
identified
mint
inscriptions
syllable
consonant
bleached

Chapter 7
decoded
ruined
tragic
repaved
divided
specializing
alabaster
grandeur
predictable
curious
gullies
formal
reservoir
unnecessary
flourishes

Chapter 8
bounty
emerged
overwhelmed
quarter
inlaid
soapstone
meditating
defaced
clan
solemn

Chapter 9
suddenly
extravagant
retreating
anxious
pipal tree
treacherous
interpret
convenient
textiles
frustratingly
strained
laden

Chapter 10
surpassing
desperate
agates
geometric
collapsed
occasionally
assumed
contagious

Chapter 11
subcontinent
dramatically
millet
hymns
generation
cosmic
peasants
deserved
recite
politician

eventually
butchered
sacrifices
untouchable
initiation
plastered
bacteria
altar
charred
purify
discriminated

Chapter 12
intricately
archery
confound
charioteer
fray
dharma
chakra
abundance
magnificent
tinkling
episode
exile
captured
triumph

Chapter 13
deeds
clarified
mandalas
guarantees
committed
charitable
cascades
pervades
decay
matted
fertility
prosperity
obstacle
embattled
lotus
detachment
represent
latrines
encouraged
emphasized

Chapter 14
luxury
abused
celibacy
fordmaker
pilgrimages
lice
vermin
sandalwood
vermilion
disgusted
enlightenment
nirvana
cremated
stupas
snobby
converted
missionary

Chapter 15
qualified
coinage
enthusiasm
contagious
decipher
documents
delta
dense
assembling
profound
impact
administer
acquainted
castes

Chapter 16
rumor
messenger
futile
adjacent
impressive
elite
turbans
exhausted
trampling
traitor
treacherous
plateau
inflicts
banyan trees
ministries

Chapter 17
magnifying
gleaming
vurgery
arthritis
celestial
manuscripts
smelting

Chapter 18
satisfaction
academy
lance
mace
centralized
established
edict
pillars
forbearance
welfare
coincidentally

Chapter 19
frail
inhabited
pomegranates
sanctifies
revolved
hermit
associate
sympathetic
renunciation
pyre

Chapter 20
vacuum
highlands
rowdy
squabbled
continent

monuments
conquest
overpower

Chapter 21
glance
thread
subgroup
expenditure
offspring
distinction
pollute
clogs
mode

Chapter 22
desirous
particles
princely
sensitive
ladies-in-waiting
infiltrated
outnumbered
unfurled
immaterial
reemphasizing
corpses
insignia

Chapter 23
grazing
barren
translations
desolate
adorned
turrets
congregated
medieval
cathedral
stained glass
lime
canvas
charcoal pencil
womb
spire
rafters
processions
garlands
devotee
incense
anointing
festive
broad
lotus
lavish

Epilogue
festivity
reborn
oasis
diverse
vegetarian
oil lamps
netherworld
buffalo
bamboo
coriander
cumin
turmeric
chutneys

MOUNTAINS AND MONSOONS: THE GEOGRAPHY OF SOUTH ASIA

CHAPTER SUMMARY

South Asia is a land of weather and geographical extremes, defined by heavy rains of the monsoon season and intense summer heat as well as the Himalayas, the highest mountain range in the world.

ACCESS

BUILDING BACKGROUND

What do you already know about the geography of South Asia? What would you like to know? In your history journal, copy the K-W-L graphic organizer from page 8 of this study guide. In the *What I Know* column, write what you already know (if you don't know anything, that's okay). In the *What I Want to Know* column, write three questions that you have. After reading the chapter, complete the *What I Learned* column with facts about the land of South Asia.

CAST OF CHARACTERS

Write a few words about why this character was important.

Valmiki (vahl-MEE-kee) _____

WHAT HAPPENED WHEN?

What happens every year in July and August in South Asia?

_____

What civilization began around 2600 BCE? _____

What national holiday is celebrated every year on January 26? _____

What happened in the Gujarat region of India on January 26, 2001?

_____

WORD BANK

monsoons   Paleolithic   basalt   millet   sorghum

Choose words from the Word Bank to complete the sentences.

1. Humans used stone tools but did not farm during the _____ period.

2. Every summer the heavy winds and rains of the _____ come to South Asia.

3. _____ and _____ are cereal grains grown in central India.

4. _____ is a soft igneous rock that enriches the central Indian soil and helps it retain water.

WORD PLAY

Prefixes: A *subcontinent* is a large area of land that is part of an even larger continent. India, for instance, is a subcontinent of Asia. The prefix *sub-* comes from Latin, and means "under," "below," or "close to." There are many words that begin with the prefix *sub-*. With a group of friends, have a contest to see who can come up with the most words that begin with *sub-*. For five minutes list all the words you can think of in your history journals, then read your lists to each other. Look up in a dictionary any words you don't know.

COMPREHENSION
SEQUENCE OF EVENTS

A series of ancient geological events caused the creation of the precious stones and metals we now mine from the layers of the earth's crust. Read the passage in the chapter on pages 22–23 that describes how such events created the stone called chalcedony, which was used by early men to create tools and transformed by later people into carnelian to make beads. Use the sequence of events graphic organizer on page 9 of this study guide to put the geological events that created chalcedony in the correct order from beginning to end.

_____ Mineral gases collected and slowly hardened to form chalcedony.

_____ Molten rocks called lava escaped through cracks in the crust.

_____ The lava cooled.

_____ The Indian landmass crashed against the Eurasian plate millions of years ago.

_____ Over millions of years the softer rock around the chalcedony wore away.

_____ Lumps of chalcedony were washed down the mountains and collected in the valleys.

_____ The lowest levels of the earth's crust were pushed up to form the Himalayas.

_____ Deeply buried layers of the earth's crust with metals and valuable rocks were brought to the earth's surface.

WORKING WITH PRIMARY SOURCES

Bead-grinding stone with beads, Mohenjo Daro, Pakistan

The ancient South Asian people probably used the beautiful beads they made as money, trading them for the things they needed. They may also have used the beads as amulets, wearing them as protection from evil. What would it be like to create your own money, in the form of beads? Or to create a magically powerful bead that would protect you?

What kinds of shapes or symbols might you use on your beads? What colors? On a page in your history journal, use colored pencils to design two beads—one for money, and one for protection. Write a paragraph that explains what colors, shapes, and symbols you used in your bead designs and why.

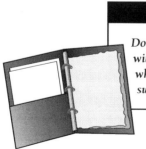

HISTORY JOURNAL

Don't forget to share your history journal with your classmates, and ask if you can see what their journals look like. You might be surprised—and get some new ideas.

STONE SERPENTS: EARLY HUMANS AND STONE AGE CULTURES

CHAPTER SUMMARY

Ancient stone tools discovered by archaeologists in the Kashmir region show that humans lived in Asia as early as 400,000 BCE. The Sanskrit legend *Nilmatha Purana* describes the beginnings of Kashmir.

ACCESS

BUILDING BACKGROUND

The first pages of the chapter describe how archaeology helped us learn about early human life in the Kashmir region. Read the passages on pages 26–27 and answer the following questions in complete sentences in your history journal.

1. Why didn't Dr. Sankalia expect to find any sign of early humans in Kashmir?

2. Why was the discovery of the hand axe so exciting?

3. Ten years later, how did the items that other archaeologists found confirm Dr. Sankalia's discovery?

CAST OF CHARACTERS

Write a complete sentence about who this person is and why he is important.

Hasmukh Sankalia _____

WHAT HAPPENED WHEN?

Write what happened on the dates below.

1969 _____

about 1100 CE _____

DO THE MATH

How many years passed between 1100 CE and 1969?

_____

WORD BANK

petroglyphs Nagas

Choose the correct word from the Word Bank to complete the sentence.

To this day, people living around Nagin Lake in Kashmir believe that _____ are serpentlike beings who live near springs and have the power to protect humans from evil spirits.

WORD PLAY

Prefixes: *Geologists*, scientists who study landforms, helped confirm Dr. Sankalia's discovery. The prefix *geo* comes from Greek, and means "earth," "ground," or "soil." A lot of words begin with *geo*. In your dictionary, find two more words that begin with *geo*. Write the words and their definitions in your history journal, and then write a complete sentence using each word.

COMPREHENSION

TIMELINE

The Kashmir region was created by a sequence of geological events that took place over millions of years. Read the description of these events on page 27, and use the timeline graphic organizer on page 9 of this study guide to match the following dates and geological events in correct order from beginning to end.

200,000 years ago	Earthquakes tilted up one side of the valley, moving the lake and exposing new land.
4,000,000 years ago	The climate warmed, and humans could live on the land all year long.
10,000 BCE	Earthquakes cracked the mountain ranges and water escaped the lake, forming the Jhelum River.
400,000 years ago	A huge lake formed when the Indian subcontinent crashed into Asia.

Answer the following question in a complete sentence.

Why did ancient people in the Nagin Lake region live there only in the summer?

WORKING WITH PRIMARY SOURCES

Nilmatha Purana, about 1100 CE

The Sanskrit legend *Nilmatha Purana,* passed down by holy men for thousands of years, tells the story of the beginning of Kashmir. Its mythology includes gods, demons, and the benevolent serpentlike beings called Nagas. Read the chapter, including the summarization of the *Nilmatha Purana* on pages 28–29, and answer the following questions.

1. When did humans begin to live year-round in the Kashmir region?

   _____ (a) about 10,000 BCE   _____ (c) 1969

   _____ (b) about 4,000,000 years ago   _____ (d) about 400,000 BCE

2. What happened that enabled humans to begin to live year-round in Kashmir?

   _____ (a) There were glaciers.   _____ (c) People learned how to farm.

   _____ (b) People began to make toos.   _____ (d) The climate warmed.

3. When was the *Nilmatha Purana* written down?

   _____ (a) about 400,000 BCE   _____ (c) about 10,000 BCE

   _____ (b) about 1100 CE   _____ (d) 1969

4. How many years passed between the approximate time that people began to live year-round in the Kashmir region, and the writing of the *Nilmatha Purana*?

   _____ (a) about 11,100 years   _____ (c) about 400,000 years

   _____ (b) about 4,000,000 years   _____ (d) about 100,000 years

MAKING INFERENCES

In the *Nilmatha Purana,* the goddess of the lake put a curse on the land so that it could only be used six months a year for "four long ages." Through archaeology and geology, we now know that from about 400,000 BCE to about 10,000 BCE (almost 400,000 years), people were indeed only able to live on the land during the warmer months of the year. The legend *Nilmatha Purana* was written almost 10,000 years after people first began to be able to live year-round in the Kashmir region. Answer the following questions in complete sentences in your history journal.

1. How do you think the ancient people who wrote the *Nilmatha Purana* in 1100 CE could possibly have known of the prehistoric "four long ages" when the land was only partially habitable by humans?

2. Do you think we will ever be able to solve this mystery? Explain your answer.

FARMERS AND HERDERS: NEOLITHIC TIMES

CHAPTER SUMMARY

The development of agriculture and the domestication of animals during the Neolithic period reduced the need for ancient South Asian people to wander and enabled them to create settled communities.

ACCESS

The ancient South Asians depended on plants and animals for food. What kinds of food did they eat? Using the main idea map graphic organizer on page 8 of this study guide, create a map with two large circles. In one circle, write *Plants*, in the other, *Animals*. As you read the chapter, in the connecting smaller circles write the different kinds of plants and animals raised by the ancient South Asians, and the kinds of food they made from these sources.

WHAT HAPPENED WHEN?

Fill in the blanks as you read the chapter.

The Neolithic period in South Asia began about _____ years ago. It lasted from

_____ BCE to _____ BCE.

WORD BANK

domestication   Neolithic   analogy

Choose words from the Word Bank to complete the sentences.

1. Historians use _____ to make informed assumptions about the distant past.
2. The _____ of animals lessened early human dependence on hunting.
3. During the _____ period, South Asians began to settle into villages.

CRITICAL THINKING
CAUSE AND EFFECT

Archaeology has revealed a great deal about South Asia in Neolithic times. In your history journal, create a cause and effect graphic organizer similar to the T-chart on page 9 of this study guide Below is a list of causes and effects related to South Asian archaeology. As you read the chapter, match the causes with their corresponding effects in the columns of your graphic organizer.

CAUSE	EFFECT
Smaller animal bones were found,	SO historians are able to figure out a lot about their daily lives.
Archaeologists found evidence of the same kinds of tools used in both mountain camps and villages,	SO we don't have any written records of their lives.
Houses, tools, weapons, and garbage were left behind by the ancient South Asians,	SO we know that people made their living by herding sheep, cattle, and goats.
Neolithic South Asians couldn't write,	SO it is possible that the same people lived in both places.

COMPREHENSION
OUTLINE

The chapter tells the story of what year-round life might have been like for a Neolithic South Asian family. Use the outline graphic organizer on page 8 of this study guide to more fully understand how people survived in those challenging times. Write the main subject of the outline at the top of the page, and then write several details from the chapter beneath each of the following topics.

Topic I: Summer in the mountains and preparation for the harvest

Topic II: Harvesting the wild grain and taking it home

Topic III: Home repairs

Topic IV: Planting and protecting the fields

DRAWING CONCLUSIONS

Ancient people in the Neolithic period made changes that greatly improved their lives. Answer the following questions in complete sentences.

1. What was the one thing people needed to develop so that they could stop hunting and gathering, and live in one place?

   _____

   _____

2. What were some of the benefits of living in one place?

   _____

   _____

3. Why do anthropologists call the development of agriculture the "Agricultural Revolution"?

   _____

   _____

4. Did the people who lived during the Agricultural Revolution know that the changes they were making would have such an enormous impact on future human life?

   _____

   _____

GROUP TOGETHER

Wouldn't it be fun to know what other students think about what Jana's life might have been like? How would it have differed from your life today? Get a few friends together and ask your teacher to help you organize a discussion group at school. Have one person take notes and another person present the group's ideas to the class.

GADGETS GALORE: THE BEGINNINGS OF TECHNOLOGIES AND TRADE

CHAPTER SUMMARY

The ancient South Asian people developed technologies that enabled them to make clay pots and other items that encouraged trade and the growth of towns and villages.

ACCESS

WITH A PARENT OR PARTNER

The invention of clay pots revolutionized food preparation and storage in ancient South Asia. Think about the technologies we have today that make getting food and preparing a meal possible. In your history journal, create a three-column chart with the following titles: *Getting Food*, *Storing Food*, and *Preparing Food*. With a parent or another older family member, write under each category several machines and technologies we use today to help us put dinner on the table.

WHAT HAPPENED WHEN?

Write in a complete sentence what happened on the following dates.

about 5500 BCE _____

about 3500–3300 BCE _____

about 2800 BCE _____

GO FIGURE

Did 2800 BCE come before or after 5500 BCE? _____

WORD BANK

bangles   ore

Choose words from the Word Bank to complete the sentences.

1. Very hot fires were used to extract copper from _____.

2. Ancient South Asians wore and traded bracelets, or _____, made from shell.

WORD PLAY

The types of clay pots made by the ancient South Asians and by some potters today are sometimes called *terracotta*. Look up the word *terracotta* in your dictionary and answer the following questions.

1. What language does the word *terracotta* come from? _____

2. What is the literal two-word English translation of *terracotta*? _____

3. What mix of two colors is sometimes called *terracotta*? _____

COMPREHENSION
SEQUENCE OF EVENTS

How did a lump of river mud become a sturdy, waterproof clay pot? Listed below are the steps ancient South Asian potters and artisans would have taken to create a pot. Read the chapter and use the sequence of events graphic organizer on page 9 of this study guide to reorganize the steps into correct order from the beginning to the end of the process.

_____ An artisan coated the inside or outside of the pot with slip.

_____ The potter sliced the pot off the wheel with a tightly held piece of thread.

_____ The potter shaped the clay on the wheel into a pot.

_____ The pot was fired in a kiln.

_____ The artisan decorated the pot with red, brown, black, or white slip.

DRAWING CONCLUSIONS

Answer the following questions in complete sentences.

1. Before the kiln was invented, how were clay pots fired?

_____

_____

2. What might an artisan have done to make a pot especially beautiful?

_____

_____

3. What else did potters make from clay? For what purpose?

_____

_____

4. Why do archaeologists believe that women made the first coiled clay pots?

_____

_____

5. When did men begin making pots, instead of women? Why?

_____

_____

WRITE ABOUT IT

Trade spread across ancient South Asia as artisans and craftsmen invented technologies to help them create beautiful and useful items such as clay pots, copper pins, shell jewelry, and stone beads. Imagine that you are a merchant in the ancient village of Mehrgarh, Pakistan. Write an advertisement for the local paper that describes the items you are selling. Using details from the chapter, describe what your items look like, where they were made, how they were made, and from what materials. You might even wish to include a "price" for each item by indicating what kinds of things you would trade for it, such as food, items of clothing, animals, or household necessities.

What are two reasons why ancient South Asian craftspeople wanted to live in larger villages and towns?

_____

_____

READ MORE

To read more about trade and technology in ancient South Asia, see the Further Reading suggestions at the end of *The Ancient South Asian World*.

5
WALLS AND WELLS:
THE FIRST CITIES OF THE INDUS

CHAPTER SUMMARY

Although it left behind no major human achievements or historical events, the Indus civilization was well organized and thrived for hundreds of years.

ACCESS

Archaeologists have learned a great deal about the Indus Civilization from the ruins of the city of Harappa in Pakistan. The chapter tells us that the city was built in a good location; use the main idea map graphic organizer on page 8 of this study guide to help you learn more about why this was so. In the large circle, write *Harappa*. In the connecting smaller circles, write words and phrases from the paragraph on page 43 that describes the location of Harappa and its benefits.

CAST OF CHARACTERS

In your history journal, answer the following questions in complete sentences.

1. Who was Alexander Cunningham?

2. What was he hoping to find in the mounds of the Punjab?

3. What did he find, and what was its significance?

WHAT HAPPENED WHEN?

Use the timeline graphic organizer on page 9 of this study guide to arrange the following dates from the chapter in chronological order and describe what happened on each date.

early 1850s	about 500 BCE	early 1920s
1893	about 2600 BCE	about 1900 BCE

WORD BANK

caravanserai   courtyard

Complete the sentence below with the correct word from the Word Bank.

Traders visiting Harappa stayed in a _____, a place outside the city walls where they could store the goods they didn't want to take into the city to sell.

WORD PLAY

Prefixes: The prefix *uni* in the word *unicorn* comes from Latin and means "one." What other words begin with *uni*? List as many words as you can think of in your history journal, then in your dictionary find three more words that begin with *uni*. Write those words and their definitions in your history journal, then write each word in a complete sentence.

CRITICAL THINKING

Harappa was a very organized and well-developed city. Read the chapter and put a checkmark beside any of the following features you might expect to find in ancient Harappa.

_____ suburbs   _____ gateways

_____ offices   _____ markets

_____ sidewalks   _____ craft workshops

_____ four-story buildings   _____ drainage systems

_____ public parks   _____ hotels

_____ warehouses

WITH A PARENT OR PARTNER

The image on the stone seal discovered by Alexander Cunningham at Harappa was that of a unicorn. We do not know the symbolic meaning of the unicorn to the people of the Indus civilization, but the unicorn is a fascinating mythical creature that appears in the art and legends of many cultures. One of the most famous and intriguing examples of the unicorn in art can be found in the Unicorn Tapestries housed at the Cloisters, a branch of the Metropolitan Museum of Art in New York City. In these extraordinarily beautiful woven wall hangings, medieval Europeans used the unicorn symbolically to tell a story that may have had underlying religious meaning, or may simply have been a tale of courtly love. You can learn more about the Unicorn Tapestries online at *www.metmuseum.org/explore/Unicorn/unicorn_inside.htm*. With a parent or older family member, look at the series of pictures of the tapestries and read their descriptions. Then, in your history journal write a paragraph that describes your thoughts about the hunt of the unicorn. Do you find the story and images beautiful? Sad? Mysterious? Also answer the following questions:

1. What possible meanings do you think the unicorn may have had to the ancient people of Harappa?

_____

_____

2. Why do you think they put the unicorn on their seal?

_____

_____

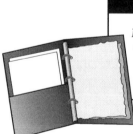

HISTORY JOURNAL

Don't forget to share your history journal with your classmates, and ask if you can see what their journals look like. You might be surprised—and get some new ideas.

SCRATCHES, SEALS, AND SYMBLS: THE BIRTH OF WRITING

CHAPTER SUMMARY

Writing began in the Indus Valley as markings on ancient pottery, and developed into the Indus script that archaeologists today are still trying to understand. Many of the examples we have of Indus script are inscriptions on ancient seals.

ACCESS

What do you know about the development of writing in the Indus Valley? What would you like to know? Use the K-W-L graphic organizer on page 8 of this study guide to explore these subjects. In the *What I Know* column, write everything you already know on the subject (if you don't know anything, that's okay). Fill in the *What I Want to Know* column with your questions, and as you read the chapter, write the answers to your questions and other interesting facts in the *What I Learned* column.

WHAT HAPPENED WHEN?

In complete sentences, write what happened on the following dates.

about 4500 BCE _____

about 4000 BCE _____

about 3300 BCE _____

about 2800–2600 BCE _____

WORD BANK

shards   steatite   graffiti   faience

Use words from the Word Bank to complete the sentences. One word is not used.

1. Many finished pieces of pottery were found by archaeologists with symbols scratched into them, called _____.

2. _____, or soapstone, was bleached with a hardening solution before being made into seals.

3. _____ was a glassy paste made from ground quartz that could be molded into seals, then fired and glazed.

WORD PLAY

Look up in a dictionary the word you did not use. Write a sentence using that word in your journal.

CRITICAL THINKING

COMPARE AND CONTRAST

What did Indus script share with the written language of the ancient Sumerians? What similarity does it have with Urdu, the modern language of Pakistan? Create a three-circle Venn diagram in your history journal, similar to the Venn diagram graphic organizer on page 9 of this study guide. Label one circle *Indus script*. Label the second circle *Urdu*, and the third *Sumerian*. As you read the chapter, write the words or phrases below in the correct circles. Write any details that are shared by any of the languages in the shaded areas where the circles connect with each other.

- 2,000 examples found
- not related to any known writing system
- written from right to left
- sometimes written in *boustrophedon* style
- used both symbols and letters
- used about 450 symbols
- first used more than 700 symbols
- number of symbols later dropped to fewer than 50

FACT OR OPINION?

A fact is a statement that can be proven. An opinion is a statement that cannot be proved or disproved. Make a two-column chart in your journal. Label one column *Fact* and the other column *Opinion*. Write each fact or opinion below from the chapter in the column where it belongs.

1. A lot of the examples we have of Indus script come from inscriptions on seals.
2. The square seals of the Indus cities were made from steatite.
3. Seals were probably used only by wealthy traders, land owners, or religious leaders.
4. Seal makers bleached steatite with a chemical solution that made it hard and white.
5. The city government probably controlled seal making.
6. Seals were important symbols of power.
7. Probably only one person used a seal.
8. The ancient Indus people were very careful about getting rid of their worn-out seals.
9. Faience can be colored with copper to make it a turquoise color.
10. After a seal had been used a while, its edges would get worn and rounded.

THINK ABOUT IT

Ancient Indus seals were personal representations of identity and power. Imagine having your own seal. What would it look like? What images or symbols would be on the seal? What words would you use? Use colored pens or pencils to design a seal that uniquely represents you. Draw it in the box below.

TRASH AND TOILETS: THE CITIES OF THE INDUS

CHAPTER SUMMARY

Harappa, Mohenjo Daro, and Dholavira were the three major cities of the Indus. They had similarities in their architecture and street layouts that lead archaeologists to believe that they may have shared government by one person or a group of people.

ACCESS

The cities of Harappa and Mohenjo Daro, located in what is now Pakistan, had several strong similarities that are described on pages 51–52. As you read the first few pages of the chapter, in your history journal make a list of five features the cities shared. Then answer the questions below in your journal in complete sentences.

1. Why did people in ancient cities build on top of the ruins of old buildings?

2. What are some of the reasons people might not have lived in Harappa or Mohenjo Daro year-round?

CAST OF CHARACTERS

What two areas of study does archaeologist Professor Heather M.-L. Miller specialize in?

WHAT HAPPENED WHEN?

What architectural feature of Mohenjo Daro was built about 2000 BCE?

WORD BANK

fragment   orientation

Choose the correct word from the Word Bank to complete the sentence.

The _____, or direction, of streets in the cities of the Indus were strangely similar.

WORD PLAY

What do you think the word *pyrotechnics* means? The interview at the end of the chapter tells us one way the word is used in archaeology, but there is another, more common meaning for the word. The prefix *pyr*, which comes from Greek, gives us a clue. Look up *pyrotechnics* in your dictionary and answer the following questions.

1. What is the meaning of the prefix *pyr*? _____

2. How does your dictionary define *pyrotechnics*? _____

3. How or when have you experienced *pyrotechnics*? _____

_____

CRITICAL THINKING
OUTLINE

The Indus cities of Harappa, Mohenjo Daro, and Dholavira were alike in some important ways but had distinct differences, too. Use the outline graphic organizer on page 8 of this study guide to help you understand the unique features of these intriguing ancient cities. Write the main idea of your outline at the top of the page, and then write several details from the chapter beneath each of the following topics.

Topic I: Features of Harappa

Topic II: Features of Mohenjo Daro

Topic III: Features of Dholavira

MAKING INFERENCES

What do the ruins of large palaces and temples usually tell us about an ancient culture? What does the lack of large palaces or temples in the Indus cities tell us about the ancient South Asians? How does it add to their mystery? Write a paragraph in your history journal that answers these questions.

COMPREHENSION

Read the interview with archaeologist Heather M.-L. Miller at the end of the chapter, and answer the following questions.

1. What were three unpleasant or dangerous things Professor Miller wished to avoid by choosing to work in a desert climate?

   _____

2. How does adding straw to clay pots help keep them from cracking in the high heat of the kiln?

   _____ (a)   The straw acts like glue to hold the pot together.

   _____ (b)   The straw is very cold.

   _____ (c)   The straw makes interesting designs on the pot.

   _____ (d)   The straw burns away and leaves room for the clay to expand.

3. What skill does Professor Miller say is an important part of her work as an archaeologist?

   _____ (a)   cooking

   _____ (b)   writing

   _____ (c)   driving

   _____ (d)   speaking

4. What highly individual "personal touch" has been discovered again and again on clay artifacts left behind by the ancient people of the Indus?

   _____ (a)   names

   _____ (b)   portraits

   _____ (c)   fingerprints

   _____ (d)   stories

5. What does Professor Miller believe is the really important thing about archaeology?

   _____

   _____

GOING SHOPPING: ARTS AND CRAFTS IN THE INDUS VALLEY

CHAPTER SUMMARY

The farmers, fishermen, and herders of the Indus Valley went to the cities after the harvest to celebrate and to trade their produce for goods created by craftsmen and artisans.

ACCESS

Rural people in the Indus came to the cities to shop for both necessities and luxury items made by craftsmen. What kinds of artisans did they find in the cities, and what kinds of things did the artisans make? As you read the chapter, use the main idea map graphic organizer on page 8 of this study guide to learn more about the arts and crafts of the Indus. In one central circle, write *Artisans and their Crafts*. In connecting circles, write the names of at least five types of artisans who worked in the cities; connect still smaller circles to the artisan circles, in which you write the types of crafts they produced.

WHAT HAPPENED WHEN?

In about what year does the chapter's fictional story about a boy named Sarang and his trip to Harappa take place? _____

What religion may have begun around 2600–1900 BCE of the Indus period?

_____

WORD BANK

inlay   yoga

Use words from the Word Bank to complete the sentences.

1. Indus craftsmen such as jewelers and furniture makers may have used _____ in their creations, which is a decorative filling of a different color or material.

2. _____ is an ancient practice that many people still do today for exercise, relaxation, or spiritual purposes.

WORD PLAY

The chapter tells us that Indus Valley jewelers and craftsmen made *pendants*. Look up *pendant* in your dictionary and answer the following questions in your history journal.

1. What is the definition of *pendant*, as something people wore?

2. What is another definition of *pendant*?

3. What is one of the languages that *pendant* comes from?

CRITICAL THINKING
CAUSE AND EFFECT

The table below lists causes and effects from the chapter that relate to arts and crafts trading in the Indus cities. Read the chapter, and in your history journal create a cause and effect graphic organizer similar to the T-chart on page 9 of this study guide. Match the causes with the correct effects in the columns of your graphic organizer.

CAUSE	EFFECT
Coppersmiths and potters worked on the southern edge of Harappa	SO it would have taken one worker more than 480 working days to complete a belt of 36 beads.
It took several days to drill a hole in one long bead,	SO that the sparks from their furnaces would be blown away from the crowded city streets.
The flat clay disks used to cover pots have been found to have child-sized hand- and footprints pressed into them,	SO that their goods would be protected from bandits who hid in the forest.
People traveling to the city from the country with their goods would have set up camp with other travelers	SO archaeologists believe that children helped make them.

DRAWING CONCLUSIONS

Archaeologists have found several stone sculptures in Mohenjo Daro similar to the one that is called "the Priest King." The posture of the people in the sculptures is described as "seated, with one knee bent to the ground and the other raised." We are told that people who appear to be worshiping deities on many Indus seals sit in this position. In your history journal, write a paragraph that answers the following questions.

1. What is it about the posture of the stone "priest king" statues that suggests that they were not, in fact, priest kings, but instead important clan or community leaders?

2. What kind of posture would you expect to see in a statue of a king?

WITH A PARENT OR PARTNER

The ancient practice of yoga is still used widely today by people around the world for health or spiritual purposes. Yoga combines breathing with a series of physical movements called *asanas* in ways that can promote relaxation and improve physical conditioning. One of the easiest and most important poses is called *Savasana*, or "the Corpse" pose. Usually it is performed at the end of a yoga session, with the goal of relaxed, quiet awareness. If you would like to try Savasana, follow these steps:

1. Lie on your back on the floor or a mat with your feet slightly apart, arms at your sides, and palms facing up.

2. Close your eyes and breath slowly and deeply.

3. Starting with your feet, think about the different parts of your body and imagine them relaxing and letting go of tension. Move up your body, gradually relaxing every part, all the way up to your face and head.

4. Continue to relax and breathe slowly for 5 to 10 minutes.

5. Don't fall asleep!

6. Rise slowly and gently, and enjoy the rest of your day.

If you would like to learn more about yoga, ask a parent or older family member to help you do an Internet search on the subject or find a book at the library. You can also find introductory yoga instruction on videos, or you can look in your phone book for local yoga centers that offer classes.

BY LAND AND BY SEA: TRADE WITH THE NEAR EAST

CHAPTER SUMMARY

Archaeological evidence indicates that people from the Indus Valley civilizations of about 2000 BCE traveled by sea and by land to trade their unique goods with other cultures.

ACCESS

What highly valued goods and crafts did Indus traders take to Mesopotamia? What Mesopotamian goods might they have brought back home with them? As you read the chapter, use the main idea map graphic organizer on page 8 of this study guide to learn more about the kinds of things the Indus people and the Mesopotamians traded. Create two large central circles, and in one write *Indus Trade Items*. In the other large circle, write *Mesopotamian Trade Items*. In smaller connecting circles, write the kinds of crafts, produce, precious objects, and animals that might have been offered by each culture.

CAST OF CHARACTERS

Write a complete sentence describing the significance of each of these characters.

Queen Puabi of Ur _____

King Sargon _____

WHAT HAPPENED WHEN?

When were the archaeological remains of the Indus Valley civilizations discovered?

_____

WORD BANK

quay

Have you ever heard the word *quay*? Look the word up in your dictionary and answer the following questions in your history journal.

1. What is the definition of *quay*?

2. How many possible pronunciations are there for *quay*?

3. What three-letter word sounds the same as one pronunciation of *quay*? (Hint: you use it to unlock a door.)

4. Write a complete sentence using the word *quay*.

COMPREHENSION

What route did trade boats bound for Mesopotamia take? Number the following travel sequence in correct order from first to last.

_____ The ship arrived at the delta of the Tigris and Euphrates Rivers.

_____ The captain could sail across the Arabian Sea to Oman, or sail directly north through the Persian Gulf to Mesopotamia.

_____ The ship arrived in Ur.

_____ The ship sailed west from Dholavira across the delta of the Indus River.

_____ A local fisherman was hired to help guide the ship through the channels of the Tigris and Euphrates Delta.

_____ The coast became dangerously rocky and the waters filled with sea snakes.

Answer the following questions.

1. Of these four items taken for trade in Mesopotamia, which was considered the most valuable?

_____ (a) peacocks   _____ (c) *shisham* wood

_____ (b) carnelian beads   _____ (d) cotton cloth

2. Where do we get our information about how boats of this period were constructed?

_____ (a) from paintings   _____ (c) from drawings

_____ (b) from stories   _____ (d) from seals and clay models

3. From what country might the Indus traders have brought lapis lazuli and tin?

_____ (a) Greece   _____ (c) Afghanistan

_____ (b) Mesopotamia   _____ (d) Ethiopia

ALL OVER THE MAP
INTERACTION

Complete the map below, showing trade routes between the Near East and Central Asia (2300–1900 BCE), and answer the following questions.

1. Indicate, using shading or a pattern, the area of the Indus Valley culture. Identify the shading in the legend.

2. Indicate the region of Mesopotamia with shading, and use the legend to identify the shading.

3. What natural barriers would traders have to cross to go from Shortughai to the Gulf of Kutch?

_____

4. How far would traders have to go from Nausharo to Ur if they traveled by land?
   Use the mileage scale to calculate the distance, and write it here. _____

5. How far would these traders have to go if they made some of the journey by
   sea? _____

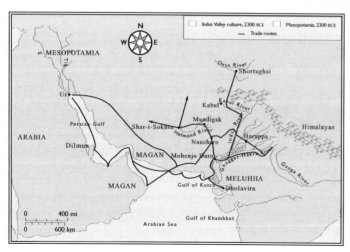

MYSTERY IN THE CITY: DECLINE AND CHANGE IN THE LATE HARAPPAN PERIOD

CHAPTER SUMMARY

Cultural changes during the late Harappan Period included new burial practices and improved methods of craft making. The gradual disappearance of the Saraswati River probably caused the decline of the Indus cities.

ACCESS

What were some of the changes and improvements developed by craftsmen during the late Harappan Period? To learn about these advances, create a two-column chart in your history journal. Label one column *Craft*, and one column *Changes*. As you read the chapter, write the names of the different types of crafts in the *Craft* column, and describe their improvements or differences in the *Changes* column. You should be able to find at least five examples of new ways of doing things in the late Harappan period.

WHAT HAPPENED WHEN?

Using the timeline graphic organizer on page 9 of this study guide, arrange the following dates from the chapter chronologically from top to bottom on the timeline, then briefly describe what happened during these approximate dates in the corresponding boxes.

about 1900 BCE   about 1200 BCE–600 BCE

about 1500 BCE–600 BCE

DO THE MATH

How many years passed between 1900 BCE and 600 BCE?

WORD BANK

intrepidly   Aryans   Indo-Aryan

Use words from the Word Bank to complete the sentences.

1. Historians originally believed that _____ invaded and destroyed the Harappan civilization, but that was probably not true.

2. In the *Rig Veda*, the rain and thunder God Indra fought _____, or bravely.

3. The language and traditions of _____ speakers eventually overwhelmed Harappan culture.

WITH A PARENT OR PARTNER

The chapter tells us that Indra was the Sanskrit god of thunder, and Zeus was the Greek god of thunder. There was a god of thunder in Norse mythology, too. With a parent or older family member, do an Internet search for information using the words "Norse mythology god of thunder." In your history journal, write a description of the Norse god of thunder in complete sentences. Include his name, who his parents were, and how, according to legend, he created thunder.

CRITICAL THINKING
OUTLINE

Burial practices changed dramatically in the Indus Valley during the late Harappan Period. Use the outline graphic organizer on page 8 of this study guide to help you more fully understand how burial changed. Write the main idea of the outline at the top of the page, and then fill in several details from the chapter beneath each of the following topics.

Topic I: Original burial practices, and how they changed at first

Topic II: Later, more drastic changes in burial practices

Topic III: Two possible reasons that burial practices changed

COMPREHENSION

Answer the following questions.

1. What do historians believe happened to the people whose unburied skeletons were found in abandoned parts of Harappa?

    _____ (a) they died in battles

    _____ (b) they died of contagious diseases

    _____ (c) they died in a great storm

    _____ (d) they were poisoned

2. About how wide across was the Saraswati River, before it began to dry up?

    _____ (a) 30 feet

    _____ (b) 5 miles

    _____ (c) 100 yards

    _____ (d) 20 miles

3. What is the meaning of the Sanskrit word *arya*? _____

4. What is the *Rig Veda*? _____

5. What was the name of the god of fire in the *Rig Veda*?

    _____ (a) Indra

    _____ (b) Zeus

    _____ (c) Osiris

    _____ (d) Agni

HISTORY JOURNAL

Don't forget to share your history journal with your classmates, and ask if you can see what their journals look like. You might be surprised—and get some new ideas.

FIRE AND SACRIFICE: LIVING BY THE VEDAS

CHAPTER SUMMARY

The Sanskrit scriptures known as the Vedas dictated the rigid, four-part class structure of the culture that began to develop in the Ganges River Valley around 2000 BCE.

ACCESS

The Vedic peoples believed that people were born into one of four different classes, depending on how well they had behaved in previous lives. These four *varna*, or classes, were said to come from the body of a cosmic being named Parusha. To learn more about the four varna, create a chart in your history journal with three columns. Label the first column *Varna*, the second column *Body of Parusha*, and the third column *Role in Society*. Write the names of the four classes in the first column. In the second and third columns, write what part of the body of Parusha each class was said to have come from, and what roles they performed in Vedic culture.

CAST OF CHARACTERS

Fill in the names of these major gods and goddesses of the Vedas:

God of war and rain _____

Sun god _____

God of fire and sacrifice _____

River goddesses (name two) _____

Creator and sustainer of the universe _____

WHAT HAPPENED WHEN?

What started to happen in the Ganges River Valley around 2000 BCE?
_____

WORD BANK

Vedas   varna   mantras

Use words from the Word Bank to complete the sentences below. One word is not used.

1. _____ are Sanskrit words or prayers that are repeated during worship.

2. The _____ are sacred writings that were originally passed on through memorization.

WORD PLAY

The chapter tells us that in the Vedas, Parusha is a *cosmic* being. What do you think the word *cosmic* means? Look up *cosmic* in your dictionary and write two of its definitions in your history journal. Then use the word in a complete sentence.

CRITICAL THINKING
CAUSE AND EFFECT

The Vedic people really believed in consequences, or cause and effect. Read the chapter, and in your history journal create a cause and effect graphic organizer similar to the T-chart on page 9 of this study guide. Below is a list of causes and effects from the chapter that relate to the different classes one might be born into in Vedic culture. Match the causes with their effects in the columns of your graphic organizer.

CAUSE	EFFECT
A person lived a perfect life,	SO they were not allowed to learn mantras.
A person did not live a good life,	SO he or she would be born into a higher class.
Ketu was born in to a priestly Brahmin family,	SO he or she would be united with the cosmic being.
A person lived a good life,	SO everyone believed that he had followed the rules of the Vedas in his last life.
The work that Shudras did was considered unclean,	SO he or she would be born into a lower class.

COMPREHENSION
SEQUENCE OF EVENTS

What were the steps taken by Brahmin priests to kindle Agni, the sacred fire, for Ketu's initiation ritual? Use the sequence of events graphic organizer on page 9 of this study guide to organize the events from the chapter in the correct order.

- After a few turns, the stick started to smoke and the charred wood powder began to glow.
- Ketu's father and the priests brought out a wood plank and a wooden drill to kindle the sacred fire.
- Agni sprang to life.
- Ketu's father pulled back and forth on the cord wrapped around the wooden drill, so that the drill pressed into the wood plank.
- A priest blew on the glowing embers and added kindling soaked in butter.

WRITE ABOUT IT

Answer the following questions in complete sentences in your history journal.

1. Why was the kitchen in a Vedic home located in the northeastern part of the house?
2. How did the rules about marriage between people from different varnas change from Vedic times to later periods?
3. What did the sacred thread that was draped around the bodies of Ketu and the other boys symbolize?
4. What were two of the reasons the Vedic peoples discriminated against the Dasa?
5. Who were the ancestors of the Dasa?

READ MORE

To read more about the Vedas and Vedic culture, see the Further Reading suggestions at the end of *The Ancient South Asian World*.

TWO GREAT ADVENTURES: EPIC TRADITIONS

CHAPTER SUMMARY

The epic story poem the *Mahabharata* tells us a great deal about the religion and culture of the Vedic peoples. The *Ramayana* is a Sanskrit story poem based on an episode from the *Mahabharata*.

ACCESS

The epic poems the *Mahabharata* and the *Ramayana* tell of intense battles between good and evil. To help you understand who the heroes and villains of these stories are, create a chart in your history journal with three columns. The first column should be labeled *Character*, the second column *Which Story*, and the third column *Description*. Write the names of each character, listed below, in the first column. As you read the chapter, in the second column write an "M" or an "R," depending on whether you discover that the character is in the *Mahabharata* or the *Ramayana*. In the third column, write a few words that describe who the character is and how he or she figures in the story.

Prince Arjuna	Lord Krishna	Bharata	Kumbakarna
Princess Draupadi	Prince Rama	Lakshmana	
the Pandavas	Sita	Ravana	
the Kauravas	Kaikeyi	Hanuman	

WHAT HAPPENED WHEN?

Write the name of the story that was written during each time period.

9th century BCE _____

7th century BCE _____

GO FIGURE

Which story was written first? _____

About how many years earlier was the first story written? _____

WORD BANK

avatar   enemy

Complete the sentence with the correct word from the Word Bank.

Lord Krishna was an _____ of the god Vishnu, who came down to earth to help Prince Arjuna.

WORD PLAY

In the *Ramayana*, the evil Ravana's brother Kumbakarna is a very heavy sleeper who must be *cudgeled* to help wake him up. Look up the noun and verb meanings of the word *cudgel* in your dictionary, and answer the following questions in complete sentences in your history journal.

1. What is a *cudgel*?

2. What does it mean to *cudgel* someone?

3. Would you like to be *cudgeled* awake? Explain your answer.

CRITICAL THINKING
OUTLINE

What is Prince Arjuna's personal conflict in the *Bhagavad Gita* portion of the *Mahabharata*? Use the outline graphic organizer on page 8 of this study guide to help you understand his struggle and its outcome. Write the main idea of your outline at the top of the page, and then write several details from the chapter beneath each of the following topics.

Topic I: Who is Prince Arjuna

Topic II: The war between the Pandavas and Kauravas, and Prince Arjuna's problem

Topic III: Lord Krishna's advice about *dharma*

Topic IV: How Lord Krishna saves the Pandavas in battle

Answer the following questions in complete sentences in your history journal.

1. Who wrote the *Ramayana*?

2. Who are the heroes of the *Ramayana*?

3. Why are monkeys considered sacred in South Asia?

ALL OVER THE MAP
INTERACTION

The *Mahabharata* provides a lot of evidence about the Vedic people, particularly about where they settled and how far they conducted trade. Do the following exercises to complete the map.

1. Use an icon to show where conch shells came from. Reference this icon in the legend.

2. Locate the site of the major battle in the Mahabharata. Identify it with an icon, and include this in your legend.

3. Label the rivers where the Vedic cities were located.

4. Label a river from the Vedic era that no longer flows.

5. Use the mileage scale to calculate how far the Vedic people had to travel from the Ganga-Yamuna Valley to collect conch shells. Write your answer here.

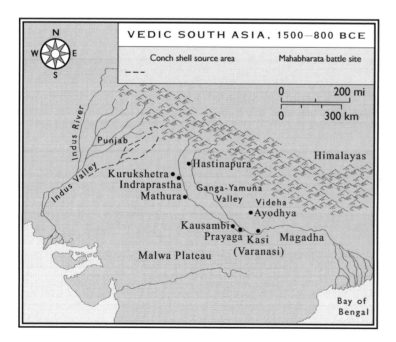

CHAPTER 13

NEW GODS: FROM BRAHMANISM TO EARLY HINDUISM

CHAPTER SUMMARY

Around 1000 BCE the religious practices and beliefs of Brahmanism began to be expanded, leading eventually to the Hindu religion.

ACCESS

The Hindu religion began to grow out of Brahmanism around 1000 BCE. What do you know about Hinduism? Who are some of the gods, and what are some of the beliefs and rituals? Use the K-W-L graphic organizer on page 8 of this study guide to help you learn more about Hinduism. In the *What I Know* column, write everything you already know on the subject (if you don't know anything, that's okay). Fill in the *What I Want to Know* column with your questions, and as you read the chapter, write the answers to your questions and other interesting facts in the *What I Learned* column.

CAST OF CHARACTERS

Write a complete sentence describing the significance of each of these characters.

Arjuna (AHR-jun) _____

Mahavira (muh-hah-VEE-ruh) _____

Siddhartha Gautama (si-DAHR-thuh GOW-tum-uh)_____

WHAT HAPPENED WHEN?

What god joined Brahma and Vishnu as one of the three major gods in about 1000 BCE?

_____

What significant religious developments occurred in the 6th century BCE?

_____

WORD BANK

karma   reincarnated   Hindus

Complete the paragraph by writing the correct words from the Word Bank in the blanks.

_____ worship the gods Vishnu, Shiva, Devi, and others. They believe in

_____, or that everyone's actions in life have good or bad consequences. If a person

has earned bad *karma*, Hindus believe that he or she might be _____, or reborn, as

an animal, rather than a human being.

CRITICAL THINKING

The Brahmins believed that the goal of life was to live so perfectly that after death you became one with *brahma*, the ultimate Supreme Being. They believed that by performing certain rituals and committing certain acts of kindness and generosity they could avoid being reincarnated and reach the level of *brahma*. In your history journal, draw a main idea map graphic organizer (see page 8 of this study guide) to help you understand this idea. In the large central circle, write *Brahmin Acts of Purification*. As you read the chapter, in smaller connecting circles write at least seven of the things Brahmins would have done during their lives to try to unite with Brahma.

COMPARE AND CONTRAST

Around 1000 BCE, Brahmins began to worship three major gods: Shiva, Vishnu, and Brahma. These gods had many differences and a few similarities. Create a Venn diagram in your history journal with three circles, similar to the graphic organizer on page 9 of this study guide. In one circle, write *Shiva*, and in the other circles write *Vishnu* and *Brahma*. Read the chapter, and write the details about each god listed below in the appropriate circles. Any characteristics shared by any of the gods should be written in the spaces where the circles of those gods overlap.

- Has three eyes
- Has a masculine and a feminine side
- Also appears as Krishna
- Rides a swan or goose
- Holds a trident
- Holds a conch shell
- Has four heads
- Is sometimes completely female, known as the Mother Goddess
- Holds a lotus
- Holds prayer beads
- Can be destructive, or loving and gentle
- "The Creator"
- "The Destroyer"
- "The Protector"

WRITE ABOUT IT

By now you know a bit about the life of a Brahmin boy training for the priesthood, or a Brahmin girl and her duties. Use information you have read in the last few chapters to write a diary entry in your history journal that imagines and describes a day in the life of a Brahmin boy or girl.

TWO GENTLE RELIGIONS: BUDDHISM AND JAINISM

CHAPTER SUMMARY

Jainism and Buddhism are two religions that began in the 6th century BCE. They teach that freedom from earthly desires is the key to spiritual enlightenment and releases human beings from the endless cycle of rebirth.

ACCESS

You have probably heard of Buddhism, one of the world's most influential religions. What do you know about Siddhartha Gautama, the founder of Buddhism? Use the K-W-L graphic organizer on page 8 of this study guide to help you learn more about Siddhartha Gautama, or "Buddha." In the *What I Know* column, write everything you already know on the subject (if you don't know anything, that's okay). Fill in the *What I Want to Know* column with your questions, and as you read the chapter, write the answers to your questions and other interesting facts in the *What I Learned* column.

CAST OF CHARACTERS

Write a complete sentence describing the significance of each of these characters.

Vardamana (vuhr-duh-MAH-nuh) (Mahavira) _____

Prashavanatha _____

Ashoka (uh-SHOK-uh) _____

WHAT HAPPENED WHEN?

Using the timeline graphic organizer on page 9 of this study guide, arrange the following dates from the chapter chronologically from top to bottom on the timeline, then briefly describe what happened during these approximate dates in the corresponding boxes.

sometime during the 6th century BCE   about 800 BCE   about 261 BCE   about 2500 BCE

WORD BANK

sangha   Eightfold Path

Complete the sentences by writing the words from the Word Bank in the blanks.

The Buddha taught that following the _____ was the way to achieve enlightenment.

He had a _____, or community of people who tried to follow his teachings and share them with others.

CRITICAL THINKING

The teachings of Prashavanatha, as taught by Mahavira, were the foundation of Jainism. Use the outline graphic organizer on page 8 of this study guide to help you more fully understand Jainism. Write the main idea of the outline at the top of the page, and then fill in several details from the chapter beneath each of the following topics.

Topic I: Vardamana's path to enlightenment

Topic II: Mahavira's five rules, and why they became popular

Topic III: Why great Jain teachers are called "ford makers"

Topic IV: Women in Jainism

Topic V: How Jains treat animals—and why

Answer the following questions in complete sentences in your history journal.

1. What is *moksha*?

2. What does the word *jina* mean?

DRAWING CONCLUSIONS

Use the main idea map graphic organizer on page 8 of this study guide to help you understand the teachings of Buddhism. Create two large central circles. In one circle, write *The Four Noble Truths*. In four smaller connecting circles, describe what the Four Noble Truths are. In the other large circle, write *The Eightfold Path*. Connect eight smaller circles to the large circle, and in each of them write one of the components of the Eightfold Path to enlightenment.

IN YOUR OWN WORDS

In the *Bhagavad Gita*, Krishna says:

> As the mountainous depths
> of the ocean
> are unmoved when waters
> rush into it,
> so the man unmoved
> when desires enter him
> attains a peace that eludes
> the man of many desires.

In your history journal, write a paragraph that restates Krishna's teaching in your own words. At the end of your paragraph, answer the following question:

Do you think it is easy for a person to find peace by controlling their desires? Explain your answer.

READ MORE

To read more about Buddhism and Jainism, see the Further Reading suggestions at the end of *The Ancient South Asian World*.

GROUP TOGETHER

Wouldn't it be interesting to know what other students think about Siddhartha's Four Noble Truths? How do they apply to today's world? Get a few friends together and ask your teacher to help you organize a discussion group at school. Have one person take notes and another person present the group's ideas to the class.

WORD FOR WORD:
EARLY HISTORIC CITIES

CHAPTER SUMMARY

Becoming part of the Persian Empire had a profound impact on the people of South Asia and on the development of its cities.

ACCESS

How did Greek and Persian influences change South Asia? What new products and practices did they bring? Read the paragraph on pages 106–107 that describes some of the ways that South Asia was changed by becoming part of the Persian Empire, and answer the following questions in your history journal in complete sentences.

1. Why were young South Asian men drafted into the Persian army?

2. What kinds of things did the soldiers see on their travels throughout the Persian Empire and Greece?

3. What new item did the foreign officials who came to Taxila from Central Asia bring with them?

CAST OF CHARACTERS

Write a complete sentence describing the significance of each of these characters.

John Prinsep _____

James Prinsep _____

Cyrus the Great of Persia _____

Challenge: What was the name of the dynasty founded by Cyrus the Great? (Hint: see Cast of Characters on page 9.) _____

WHAT HAPPENED WHEN?

In complete sentences in your history journal, describe what happened on or around the following dates.

1819   about 800–300 BCE

1780   558–529 BCE

DO THE MATH

How many years passed between 529 BCE and 1819, CE?

WORD BANK

indigo   mint   satrap

Complete the sentences by writing the words from the Word Bank in the blanks.

Coins are manufactured at a _____.

_____ is a plant that is used to make blue dye.

A _____ was a governor of a Persian state who collected taxes to send to the capital, Persepolis.

COMPREHENSION

As you read the chapter, answer the following questions.

1. What is the meaning of the Sanskrit word *danam*?

    _____ (a) coin   _____ (b) charity   _____ (c) mint   _____ (d) gift

2. What kind of metal made stronger, lighter tools and weapons?

    _____ (a) copper   _____ (b) brass   _____ (c) steel   _____ (d) iron

3. How were *castes* different from *varnas*?

    _____

4. Why did people in the Indus cities go to *ashrams*?

    _____ (a) to learn to cook   _____ (c) to compete in athletics
    _____ (b) to meditate   _____ (d) to discuss politics

WRITE ABOUT IT

The city of Taxila was a center of trade and education in the Indus. What do you think it was like to live there? Imagine that you are a resident of Taxila, and you are trying to convince a friend to come live there. What kinds of inviting things could you say about the city, its different neighborhoods, and the latest Greek and Persian innovations? Write a letter to your friend in your history journal about the luxuries and conveniences of Taxila.

ALL OVER THE MAP
LOCATION

Complete the map below showing the early states of South Asia and their capitals, 496 BCE.

1. Label these rivers:

    Narmada River   Indus River   Yamuna River   Ganga River   Brahmaputra River

2. Use shading to indicate the empire of Cyrus the Great, and key this shading in the legend.

3. Label these bodies of water:

    Arabian Sea   Bay of Bengal   Indian Ocean

4. Label the Indus Delta and the Ganga-Yamuna Delta

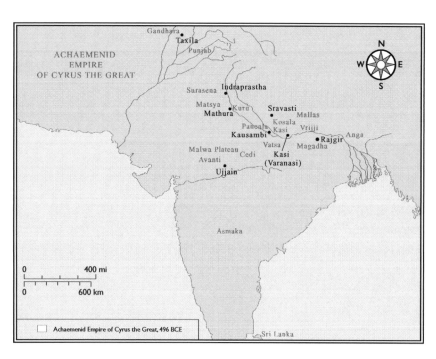

WITH FRIENDS LIKE THESE, WHO NEEDS ENEMIES? THE BEGINNINGS OF THE MAURYAN EMPIRE

CHAPTER SUMMARY

Alexander the Great's invasion of the Indus was followed by the founding of the Mauryan Empire, India's first centralized government, by Chandragupta Maurya.

ACCESS

Have you ever heard of the conqueror Alexander the Great, or Prince Chandragupta Maurya? What do you know about them? Use the K-W-L graphic organizer on page 8 of this study guide to help you learn more about these great leaders. In the *What I Know* column, write what you already know about Alexander and Chandragupta (if you don't know anything, that's okay). Fill in the *What I Want to Know* column with your questions, and as you read the chapter, write the answers to your questions and other interesting facts in the *What I Learned* column.

CAST OF CHARACTERS

In your history journal, write a complete sentence describing the significance of each of these characters.

King Ambhi (AHM-bhi)   King Porus (POHR-us)   Sikander   Arrian

Firdausi   Chandragupta (CHUN-drah-GOOP-tuh)   Kautilya (kaow-TIL-yuh)

WHAT HAPPENED WHEN?

What happened on these dates?

327 BCE _____

317 BCE _____

WORD BANK

cavalry   centralized   paladins

Complete the sentences using words from the Word Bank. One word is not used.

1. _____ were heroic knights whose stories were told in popular 13th century Persian poems.

2. In a government that is _____ one person or small group of people makes decisions for an entire country.

WORD PLAY

The chapter tells us that one king's resistance against the conquering army of Alexander the Great was *futile*. Look up *futile* in your dictionary and answer the following questions in your history journal.

1. What Latin word does *futile* come from, and what are its meanings?

2. What are two definitions of *futile*?

3. Write a complete sentence using the word *futile*.

COMPREHENSION
SEQUENCE OF EVENTS

Alexander knew that it would be difficult to defeat King Porus, who had a large, well-organized army of powerful soldiers. As you read about the conflict between Alexander and King Porus, number the following events in correct order from first to last.

_____ Alexander and his men attacked Porus's army during a heavy rainstorm.

_____ The battle lasted for more than eight hours.

_____ Alexander sent small bands of men out at night to trick Porus.

_____ Thousands of warriors and their horses and elephants were killed.

_____ Both armies were exhausted, and Alexander called a truce.

_____ Porus refused to surrender.

_____ Alexander demanded that Porus surrender at once.

_____ Porus was wounded, but he led the charge against Alexander's forces.

_____ Porus sent troops out to meet Alexander, but no one was there.

OUTLINE

Chandragupta Maurya probably could not have founded the Mauryan Empire without the help of his adviser Kautilya. In your history journal, copy the outline graphic organizer on page 8 of this study guide to help you understand their relationship. Write the main idea of the outline at the top of the page, and then fill in several details from the chapter beneath each of the following topics.

Topic I: Kautilya's theory about how to rule wisely

Topic II: Details of Chandragupta's most important improvement

Topic III: Chandragupta's ministries

WITH A PARENT OR PARTNER

The chapter tells us that Kautilya believed that kings should do anything necessary to rule their countries, even if it meant spying on their own people or assassinating their enemies. With a parent or partner, discuss the following questions. Be sure to explain your answers to each other.

1. Do you think it is right for a king to spy on his own people?

2. Do you think it is right for a king to have his enemies assassinated?

3. Can you think of any circumstances for a king or a country in which your answer might change?

GROUP TOGETHER

Wouldn't it be interesting to talk with other students think about Alexander the Great and the impact he had on the ancient world? Does he remind you of any political or military leaders from more recent times? Get a few friends together and ask your teacher to help you organize a discussion group at school. Have one person take notes and another person present the group's ideas to the class.

NOTHING BUT A ZERO: SCIENCE AND TECHNOLOGY

CHAPTER SUMMARY

Ancient Indian scientific advances in medicine, astronomy, mathematics, and metallurgy continue to have profound influence in our modern culture.

ACCESS

In what ways have we modern humans benefited from the scientific discoveries of ancient Indians? Explore this idea by creating a chart in your history journal with four columns. Label the first column *Ayurveda*, the second *Aryabhata*, the third *Zero*, and the fourth *Smelting Iron*. As you read the chapter, write a few details in each column that describe how each science, scientist, or discovery has made a lasting historical contribution.

CAST OF CHARACTERS

Answer the following questions in your history journal in complete sentences.

1. What was the name of ancient South Asia's greatest scientist?
2. What was the name of the poem he wrote?
3. What was the poem about?
4. How was the poem passed on, at first?
5. What may have happened if the poem had been written down?

WHAT HAPPENED WHEN?

What happened in 476 CE? _____

WORD BANK

Ayurveda rejuvenation

Use words from the Word Bank to complete the sentences.

Ancient Indians went to special health clinics for _____, or youthful renewal.

_____, which means "science of living," was the name of the traditional medicine practiced at these clinics.

CRITICAL THINKING
FACT OR OPINION?

A fact is a statement that can be proven. An opinion is a statement that can neither be proved nor disproved. For each statement about Ayurveda from the chapter below, write an "F" or an "O" to indicate whether it is a fact or an opinion.

_____ Ayurveda has been around for 5,000 years.

_____ A lot of people still use Ayurveda.

_____ Many Indian mothers massage their babies with oils.

_____ They believe the massages help soothe their children and prevent stomach pains.

_____ Western doctors used leeches until the beginning of the 20th century.

_____ Ayurvedic surgeons knew that patients and surgical instruments had to be clean to stop infections.

_____ Ayurvedic nursing homes were probably located outside the cities.

MAKING INFERENCES

Answer the following questions:

1. What kinds of treatments are included in Ayurveda?

_____

2. What significant idea about illness does Ayurveda teach?

_____

THINK ABOUT IT

The chapter tells us that Ayurveda didn't just try to make people feel better when they were sick, but taught good habits that helped people stay healthy. In what way is this different from modern Western medicine?

MAIN IDEA AND SUPPORTING DETAILS

Each sentence in *italics* below states a main idea from the chapter. The sentences that follow each main idea are mostly supporting ideas. Cross out the sentences that do NOT support each main idea.

1. *Even without a telescope, Aryabhata saw a lot.*
   (a) He saw that the moon was light on the side that faced the sun.
   (b) He realized that the earth and planets circled the sun.
   (c) He was very young.
   (d) He saw that the rising and setting of the sun and moon was the result of the earth turning.

2. *Aryabhata wanted his information to be easy to remember.*
   (a) He put all the numbers into a code of letters.
   (b) He watched the night sky.
   (c) He explained the code at the beginning of the poem the *Aryabhatiyam*.
   (d) He did not know about zero.

3. *Aryabhata's inventions were historically important and a great help to South Asians.*
   (a) He made a very accurate calendar.
   (b) He explained the movements of planets better than anyone else would for 1,000 years.
   (c) He was the first person to come up with an accurate measurement for pi [π].
   (d) Insects and mildew destroyed Indian manuscripts.

WRITE ABOUT IT

Write a paragraph in your history journal that explains why the Indian invention of the number zero was so historically significant.

READ MORE

To read more about the scientific advances of ancient India, see the Further Reading suggestions at the end of *The Ancient South Asian World*.

18 DHARMA, ARTHA, KAMA, AND MOKSHA: WAR AND PEACE IN THE TIME OF ASHOKA

CHAPTER SUMMARY

King Ashoka was a religious man and brilliant leader whose military victory over the eastern territory of Kalinga united it with the rest of India. He was filled with remorse over the violence of the conflict, however, and thereafter promoted the peaceful philosophy of "conquest by *dharma*."

ACCESS

The ancient Indians were highly organized and skilled at waging war. In their military academies, people of the *varnas* learned to fight with particular weapons. In your history journal, copy the main idea map graphic organizer on page 8 of this study guide to help you learn more about the weapons used by the warriors of Ashoka's time. Create a large central circle, labeled *Eight Major Weapons*. In eight smaller connecting circles, write the names of the kinds of weapons taught at the military academies.

Fill in the blanks with the correct weapon(s) used by each caste.

Brahmins _____

Kshatriya _____

Vaisya _____

Shudra _____

CAST OF CHARACTERS

Write a complete sentence that describes the significance of each character.

Ashoka (uh-SHOK-uh) _____

Bindusara (BIN-doo-SAH-rah) _____

Chandragupta (CHUN-druh-GOOP-tuh) _____

WHAT HAPPENED WHEN?

269 BCE _____

265 BCE _____

185 BCE _____

WORD BANK

dharma   artha   kama   moksha

Read the first paragraph of the chapter, in which the meanings of each of the Word Bank words are discussed. In your history journal, write a complete sentence for each word that describes its meaning.

CRITICAL THINKING
OUTLINE

King Ashoka had reasons for wanting to conquer the wealthy territory of Kalinga, but he came to regret the brutal war he waged against the Kalingans. Use the outline graphic organizer on page 8 of this study guide to help you understand what happened. Write the main idea of the outline at the top of the page, and then fill in several details from the chapter beneath each of the following topics.

Topic I: Why Ashoka wanted to conquer Kalinga

Topic II: The brutality of the war against the Kalingans

Topic III: How Ashoka felt after his victory

WORKING WITH PRIMARY SOURCES

Ashoka, Proclamation, 3rd century BCE

Read the words of Ashoka's proclamation on page 124 and answer the following questions in complete sentences in your history journal.

1. What is *dharma*?

2. Why do you think "conquest by *dharma*" became important to Ashoka after he saw the consequences of the war he had waged against the Kalingans?

MAKING INFERENCES

Ashoka wanted his people to live in ways that would lead to an "increase of their inner worthiness." What do you think he meant? Write a paragraph in your history journal that restates this part of Ashoka's proclamation in your own words. Suggest ways of living or personal choices that you think might increase one's "inner worthiness."

ALL OVER THE MAP
INTERACTION

Complete the map below, showing the extent of Ashoka's empire from 268–235 BCE, and answer the following questions.

1. Use shading to show the extent of Ashoka's empire. Identify this pattern in the legend.

2. Draw the coastal trade route and the sea trade routes on the map, and identify them in the legend.

3. Indicate on the map where the trade routes went to the east and to the west.

4. Use the mileage scale to measure the distance a coastal trader would have to travel from the mouth of the Ganga River to the city of Sopara. Write your calculation here. _____

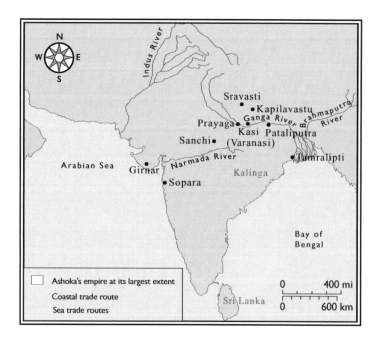

SERVICE AND STUDY: THE CYCLE OF LIFE

CHAPTER SUMMARY

Depending on whether they were male or female, ancient South Asian people had very specific roles, duties, and expectations.

ACCESS

What do you know about the lives of men and women in ancient South Asia? Use the K-W-L graphic organizer on page 8 of this study guide to help you learn more about the expectations they faced. In the *What I Know* column, write what you already know about their daily lives and duties (if you don't know anything, that's okay). Fill in the *What I Want to Know* column with your questions. As you read the chapter, write the answers to your questions and other interesting facts in the *What I Learned* column.

CAST OF CHARACTERS

Who was Ilango Adigal? Write your answer in a complete sentence.

_____

WHAT HAPPENED WHEN?

200 BCE–200 CE _____

about 1500–500 BCE _____

WORD BANK

sanctify   cremation   vegetarian

Complete the sentences with words from the Word Bank.

1. People who are _____ do not eat meat.

2. _____ is the practice of burning the body of a person who has died.

3. To _____ something is to make it sacred through performing special rituals.

WORD PLAY

Young brides in India sometimes put a streak of *vermilion* in the center part of their hair. Look up *vermilion* in your dictionary and answer the following questions in your history journal:

1. What is vermilion made of?

2. What color is vermilion?

3. What are the meanings of this sacred color, according to the description on page 130 of the chapter?

WORKING WITH PRIMARY SOURCES

Ilango Adigal, "The Ankle Bracelet," about 200 BCE–200 CE

COMPREHENSION
SEQUENCE OF EVENTS

Although ancient Indian women led mostly anonymous lives, the story "The Ankle Bracelet" tells us a lot about what the life of a married woman might have been like. After you read the details of the story on pages 126–128 of the chapter, use the sequence of events graphic organizer on page 9 of this study guide to organize the following events from the story in the correct order.

_____ The cowgirls helped Kannaki prepare a vegetarian meal for Kovalan.

_____ Kannaki washed her husband's feet.

_____ Kannaki gave Kovalan one of her bracelets to sell.

_____ Kovalan wasted all their money, so he and Kannaki decided to move and begin a new life.

_____ Kannaki lay on the sacred mountain for 14 days, grieving.

_____ They arrived at the house of some poor cowherds.

_____ The god Indra took Kannaki to heaven as a goddess, where she was reunited with Kovalan.

_____ Kovalan was killed, and the bracelet stolen.

_____ Kannaki sprinkled water on the ground and beat the soil with her palms.

_____ She served him the food, and they ate their dinner together.

DRAWING CONCLUSIONS

Answer the following questions in complete sentences.

1. Why don't people who practice the Jain religion eat after sunset?

_____

_____

2. What are some of the ways that ancient Indians displayed respect for each other?

_____

_____

3. Could people from different castes touch each other?

_____

_____

4. Why do we have to look for information about ancient South Asian women in stories like "The Ankle Bracelet," rather than in historical accounts?

_____

_____

OUTLINE

The lives of ancient South Asian men were divided into four stages. Use the outline graphic organizer on page 8 of this study guide to explore these stages. Give the outline a title, and then fill in several details from the chapter beneath each of the following life stages. Be sure to include information about when the stage began, and what the expectations were for a man in that stage of life.

Stage I: Student

Stage II: Parent

Stage III: Hermit

Stage IV: Renouncer

WHO'S IN CHARGE HERE, ANYWAY? AN AGE OF RELIGIOUS AND POLITICAL CONFUSION

CHAPTER SUMMARY

After the death of Ashoka, many groups and leaders struggled for control of South Asia. Kanishka, a great leader from Central Asia, eventually united South Asia and promoted a new form of Buddhism to attract followers.

ACCESS

Buddhism changed greatly in South Asia during the rule of Kanishka. To begin to understand why this was so, read pages 132–134 of the chapter, then answer the following questions in complete sentences in your history journal.

1. What were some Hindu beliefs and practices shared by ancient South Asians?

2. How had the Buddha been remembered and honored in the four hundred years since his death?

3. Was the Buddha considered to be a god?

4. Why did people want more than just monuments and the example of Buddha's life to follow?

5. Why did some people no longer want to pay Brahmin priests to make sacrifices for them?

CAST OF CHARACTERS

Who was Kanishka (kuh-NISH-kuh)? Write your answer in a complete sentence.

WHAT HAPPENED WHEN?

Using the timeline graphic organizer on page 9 of this study guide, arrange the following dates from the chapter chronologically from top to bottom on the timeline, then briefly describe what happened during these approximate dates in the corresponding boxes.

232 BCE   2nd century BCE   about 200 CE   end of 3rd century BCE

WORD BANK

bodhisattva

A *bodhisattva* is a

(a) mound built to hold a container of the Buddha's ashes.

(b) coin with an image of Kanishka on one side and the Buddha on the other side.

(c) being of perfect knowledge who unselfishly helps others to become like him/her.

(d) release from the cycle of rebirth.

WORD PLAY

Both Ashoka and Kanishka were rulers who were *tolerant* about religion. What does this mean? Look up the words *tolerance* and *tolerant* in your dictionary. Write the definitions of the words in your history journal, then write a complete sentence for each.

CRITICAL THINKING

Ashoka and Kanishka were leaders with some similarities. Create a Venn Diagram in your history journal with two circles, similar to the graphic organizer on page 9 of this study guide. In one circle, write *Ashoka*, and in the other circle write *Kanishka*. Read the chapter, and write the details about each ruler listed below in the appropriate circle. Any characteristics shared by Ashoka and Kanishka should be written in the space where the circles overlap.

- Ambitious
- His empire grew quickly
- Built stupas and stone monuments to Buddha
- Helped create "Theravada" Buddhism
- Loved fighting
- Met with Buddhist monks to discuss new ways of teaching Buddhism
- Loved learning new things
- Sent missionaries throughout South Asia to spread Buddha's message
- Helped create "Mahayana" Buddhism
- Wanted to share Buddhism with his people

WORKING WITH PRIMARY SOURCES

Kalishka Kushana coin, 2nd century CE

Look at the photographs of the Kalishka Kushana coin on page 135, and read the description in the text. Then answer the following questions in complete sentences in your history journal.

1. What features of his coins did Kanishka borrow from the Greeks and Romans?
2. What words sometimes accompanied the picture of Kanishka on the coins?
3. What other gods and leaders appear on the second side of some coins?

BE CREATIVE

Imagine having the power to design your own money. What would your personal coin look like? In the circles below, draw a design of your own coin, using symbols and pictures that are meaningful to you. Be sure to show both sides of the coin.

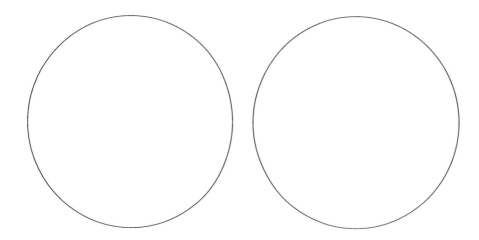

A PLACE FOR EVERYONE: CASTE AND SOCIETY

CHAPTER SUMMARY

When ancient South Asian society became more multicultural and disorganized, Brahmins introduced the Code of Manu, a set of religious rules that organized people of the four varnas into work-related subgroups called *castes*.

ACCESS

Refresh yourself on the meanings of the following terms by matching the words with their definitions or descriptions.

1. *dharma*
2. *varnas*
3. caste
4. Vedas
5. *karma*
6. the *Mahabharata*

a. the four religious classes to which people belonged

b. the spiritual consequences of one's actions

c. the sacred hymns that the Brahmins considered a handbook to life

d. one's duty, purpose, or special calling in the world

e. epic sacred poem

f. work-related subgroups of the four *varnas*

CAST OF CHARACTERS

According to Brahmin legend, who was Manu? Write your answer in a complete sentence.

_____

WHAT HAPPENED WHEN?

What is the name of the text people began to live by in the 1st century CE?

_____

WORD BANK

purify

Look up the words *purify* and *purification* in your dictionary. Write the definitions of the words below, then write a complete sentence for each.

_____

_____

_____

_____

CRITICAL THINKING
CAUSE AND EFFECT

Read the chapter, and in your history journal create a cause and effect graphic organizer similar to the T-chart on page 9 of this study guide. Below is a list of causes and effects from the chapter that relate to caste and society. Match the causes with their effects in the columns of your graphic organizer.

CAUSE	EFFECT
A person made a lot of mistakes in his last life resulting in bad *karma*,	SO that his good *karma* would help make his next life better.
The "clacking" noise of wooden shoes was heard coming down the street,	SO Brahmins were not allowed to use leather, even for their shoes.
By 1 CE, society was beginning to fall apart,	SO he became ritually unclean.
Leather could not be purified by fire,	SO the Brahmins introduced the Code of Manu to help organize society.
A person behaved well in his current life,	SO he was born a Shudra, the lowest *varna*, in the next life.
A person did not follow the actions or rituals of his caste,	SO people of other castes moved out of the way to let the Brahmin pass by without touching him.

COMPREHENSION

In ancient South Asian culture, you could sometimes identify which *varna* or caste a person belonged to by what trade he was practicing or what color she was wearing. Create a chart in your history journal with four columns. Label each column with the names of the four *varnas*—*Shudra*, *Vaisyas*, *Kshatriya*, and *Brahmin*. As you read the chapter, write the details of the *varnas* below in the correct columns.

- warriors
- wore black
- wore the sacred thread
- gold workers
- priests
- wore white
- existed to serve the other three varnas
- traders
- wore yellow
- wore only wrapped, not stitched, clothing
- wore red
- kings
- could make animal sacrifices

SOUTH ASIA'S GOLDEN AGE:
THE GUPTA EMPIRE

CHAPTER SUMMARY

The Guptas were a dynasty of rulers who strengthened the caste system and introduced local leaders called Maharajahs to the system of governance.

ACCESS

Do you have a nickname? Nicknames were important in Gupta times. They revealed a lot about their owners—and the qualities for which their owners wanted to be known. Two of Samudra Gupta's nicknames were "King of Poets" and "Uprooter of Kings." If you could give yourself or your best friend a new nickname based on personal qualities, what would it be? Write your thoughts and reasoning in your history journal.

CAST OF CHARACTERS

The Gupta Empire featured a colorful cast of characters. As you read the chapter, write a sentence that describes each of the following characters in your history journal.

Chandra Gupta (CHUN-druh GOOP-tuh)   Samudra Gupta (suh-MOO-druh GOOP-tuh)

Fa Hien (fah-HYEN)   Kumara Gupta

Kalidasa (KAH-li-DAH-sah)   Kautilya (kaow-TIL-yuh)

Rama Gupta (RAHM-uh GOOP-tuh)   Chandra Gupta II (CHUN-druh GOOP-tuh)

Xuanzang (shwen-dzang)   Skanda Gupta (SKUHN-duh GOOP-tuh)

WHAT HAPPENED WHEN?

State in a complete sentence what happened on each date.

320 CE _____

376 CE _____

5th century CE _____

WORD BANK

Maharajahs   dynasties

Choose the correct word from the Word Bank to complete the sentence.

Samudra Gupta decided to let local leaders called _____ make some of the decisions in the kingdom.

CRITICAL THINKING

Chandra Gupta II was an especially interesting Gupta ruler who reinforced the caste system. Use the outline graphic organizer on page 8 of this study guide to help you more fully understand his contributions and the life that certain people in Gupta society led. Write the main idea of the outline at the top of the page, and then fill in several details from the chapter beneath each of the following topics.

Topic I: The heroism of Chandra Gupta II

Topic II: Ways in which Chandra Gupta II fulfilled his dharma

Topic III: The life of the Chandalas (Untouchables)

WITH A PARENT OR PARTNER

The sidebar on page 146 describes the water clock that kept time in the Gupta court. In what other ways have humans tracked time through the ages? With a parent or older family member, do an Internet search for information using the phrase "the history of telling time." Then write a paragraph in your history journal that describes at least two other devices ancient humans used to tell time.

WORKING WITH PRIMARY SOURCES
WRITE ABOUT IT

Visakhadatta, *Devi-Chandraguptam*, 4th century CE

In the story of Chandra Gupta II's heroic rescue of the queen, a nervous soldier warned Chandra Gupta II that the enemy outnumbered them. Chandra Gupta II replied, "For a heroic person, number is immaterial." What do you think Chandra Gupta II meant? Write a paragraph in your history journal that explains Chandra Gupta II's words and rephrases them in your own words.

ALL OVER THE MAP
REGIONS

Complete the map of the Gupta Empire (320–540 CE) below, and answer the following questions.

1. Label the major rivers that bordered the Gupta Empire.

2. Use a pattern or shading to indicate the boundaries of the Gupta Empire, and identify this in the legend.

3. Indicate, with shading, the areas allied with the Gupta Empire.

4. Which bodies of water bordered the Gupta Empire?

   _____

5. Use the mileage scale to calculate how far the empire stretched.

   a) from east to west: _____

   b) from north to south: _____

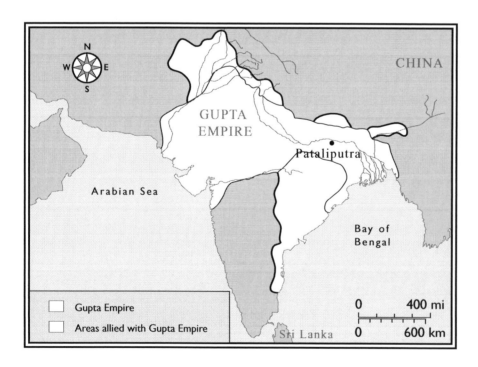

23 GODS AND CAVES: LITERATURE AND ART OF THE GUPTA ERA

CHAPTER SUMMARY

The Gupta devotion to beauty can be seen in the cave paintings, temple statuary, and architecture of the era. Chinese Buddhist monk Xuanzang wrote of the Gupta culture in his book *A Record of the Western Regions*.

ACCESS

What do you know about the art and writings of the Gupta era? Use the K-W-L graphic organizer on page 8 of this study guide to help you learn more. In the *What I Know* column, write what you already know about the art and literature of ancient India (if you don't know anything, that's okay). Fill in the *What I Want to Know* column with your questions. As you read the chapter, write the answers to your questions and other interesting facts in the *What I Learned* column.

CAST OF CHARACTERS

As you read the chapter, write three facts you discover about Xuanzang (shwen-dzang) in complete sentences.

1. _____
2. _____
3. _____

WHAT HAPPENED WHEN?

627 CE _____

WORD BANK

oasis   mudras   monastery

Complete the sentences using the correct word from the Word Bank. One word is not used.

1. _____ are symbolic hand movements with religious meanings.

2. An _____ is an area in a desert where water can be found.

WORD PLAY

Look up in a dictionary the word you didn't use. Write a sentence with that word that clearly shows its meaning.

COMPREHENSION
SUMMARIZING

Use the chart on page 154 to help you match the religious writings below with their descriptions.

a. Mahabharata   b. Tripitaka   c. Vedas   d. Ramayana

e. Panchatantra   f. Jatakas   g. Puranas   h. Sutras

_____ Hindu myths for ordinary people

_____ Buddhist sermons

_____ Explains what a *bodhisattva* is

_____ Stories for children about animals

_____ Stories about Buddha that explain what *karma* is

_____ The oldest Hindu scriptures, including the Rig Veda

_____ Poem about Prince Arjuna

_____ Story of Prince Rama and his wife Sita

CRITICAL THINKING
FACT OR OPINION?

A fact is a statement that can be proven. An opinion is a statement that can neither be proved nor disproved. Read the chapter, and for each statement about Xuanzang below, write an "F" or an "O" to indicate whether it is a fact or an opinion.

_____ It was against the law for Xuanzang to leave China and cross the desert.

_____ Xuanzang stayed in India for 13 years.

_____ Xuanzang probably would have said that his time at the University of Nalanda was the most important part of his trip.

_____ Xuanzang may have visited the Ajanata caves at some point in his studies.

_____ If Xuanzang visited the caves today, he probably would not be studying Buddhism, but life at the Gupta court.

_____ Xuanzang took 657 Buddhist texts back to China with him.

_____ Xuanzang translated the texts from Sanskrit into Chinese.

READ MORE

To read more about the literature and art of ancient India, see the Further Reading suggestions at the end of *The Ancient South Asian World*.

HISTORY JOURNAL

Don't forget to share your history journal with your classmates, and ask if you can see what their journals look like. You might be surprised—and get some new ideas.

REPORTS AND SPECIAL PROJECTS

There's always more to find out about ancient South Asia. Take a look at the Further Reading section at the end of the book (pages 163–164). Here you'll find numerous books relating to early South Asian history and culture. Many of them will be available in your school or local public library.

GETTING STARTED

Explore the Further Reading section for any of these reasons.

— You're curious and want to learn more about a particular topic.

— You want to do a research report on ancient South Asia.

— You still have questions about something covered in the book.

— You need more information for a special classroom project.

What's the best way to find the books that will help you the most?

LOOK AT THE SUBHEADS

The books are organized by topic. The subhead Religion tells you where to find books on Hinduism and Buddhism, for example. Go to Art and Architecture to learn more about Indian and Southeast Asian art. Let the subheads give you ideas for reports and special projects.

LOOK AT THE BOOK TITLES

The titles of the books can tell you a lot about what's inside. The books listed under Literature and Myths offer modern translations of some of the ancient South Asian epic stories you have learned about in the chapters.

LOOK FOR GENERAL REFERENCES

This section also lists general books, which are useful starting points for further research. General Works on Ancient South Asia will list titles that provide a broad overview of ancient South Asian history. Judge by the titles which books will be the most useful to you. Other references include:

— Dictionaries

— Encyclopedias

— Atlases

OTHER RESOURCES

Information comes in all kinds of formats. Use the book to learn about primary sources. Go to the library for videos, DVDs, and audio materials. And don't forget about the Internet!

AUDIO-VISUAL MATERIALS

Your school or local library can offer documentary videos and DVDs on ancient South Asia, as well as audio materials. If you have access to a computer, explore the sites listed on the section titled Websites (page 165) for some good jumping-off points. These are organized by topic, with brief descriptions of what you'll find on the site. Many websites list additional reading, as well as other Internet sites you can visit.

What you've learned about the ancient South Asian world so far is just a beginning. Learning more is an ongoing adventure!

LIBRARY / MEDIA CENTER RESEARCH LOG

NAME _____

DUE DATE

What I Need to **Find**

I need to use:
- ☐ primary sources.
- ☐ secondary

Brainstorm: Other Sources and Places to Look

Places I **Know** to Look

WHAT I FOUND

Rate each source from 1 (low) to 4 (high) in the categories below

helpful   relevant

How I Found it
- Suggestion
- Library Catalog
- Browsing
- Internet Search
- Web link

- Primary Source
- Secondary Source

Title/Author/Location (call # or URL)

- Book/Periodical
- Website
- Other

36101257R00037

Made in the USA
Lexington, KY
07 October 2014